(40) FUN EASY *Ukelele* SONGS

FOR KIDS+ BEGINNERS

TABLE OF CONTENTS

READING UKELELE CHORDS

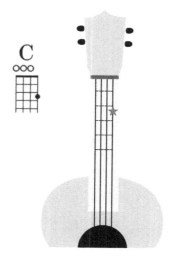

The chord diagram shows which fingers to place where. Where you see a solid circle is where you place your finger.

It shows the top 5 frets of the ukelele as if it was standing upright and you looked straight at it.

For example, for "C" Chord shown here, you would place your finger on the third fret of the A string (where the star is), then strum all strings.

READING UKELELE TABS

Each tab line represents a string on the ukelele:

A — 1ST STRING (CLOSEST TO YOR WAIST)
E — 2ND STRING
C — 3RD STRING
D — 4TH STRING (CLOSEST TO YOUR HEAD)

The number on a string represents which fret to place your finger.

For example, 0 means no fingers (just pluck the string) and 1 means place your finger on the first fret then pluck the string.

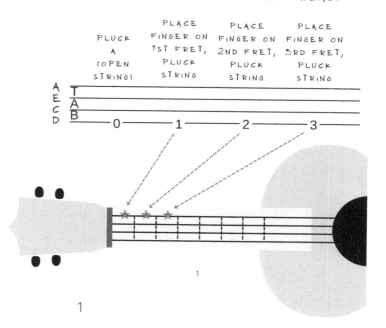

PLUCK A (OPEN STRING) — PLACE FINGER ON 1ST FRET, PLUCK STRING — PLACE FINGER ON 2ND FRET, PLUCK STRING — PLACE FINGER ON 3RD FRET, PLUCK STRING

0 — 1 — 2 — 3

RAIN, RAIN, GO AWAY

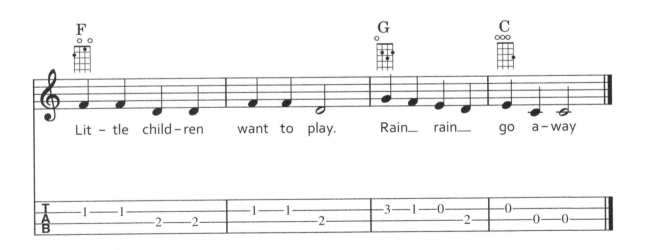

THIS OLD MAN

This old man, he played one, he played knick – knack

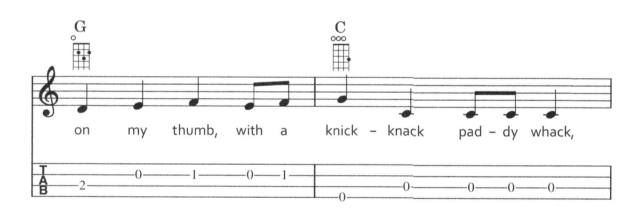

on my thumb, with a knick – knack pad – dy whack,

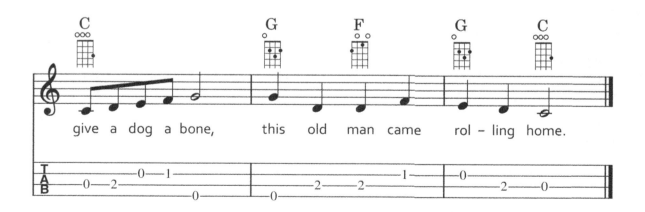

give a dog a bone, this old man came rol – ling home.

A Tisket, A Tasket

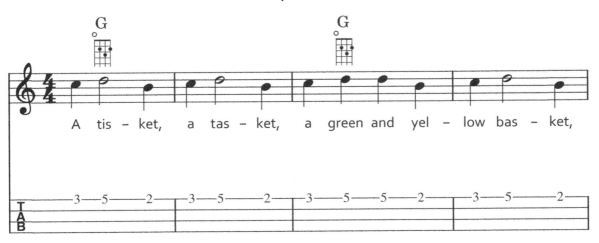

A tis – ket, a tas – ket, a green and yel – low bas – ket,

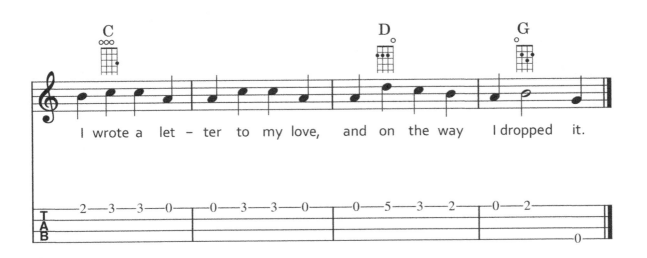

I wrote a let – ter to my love, and on the way I dropped it.

4

AURA LEE

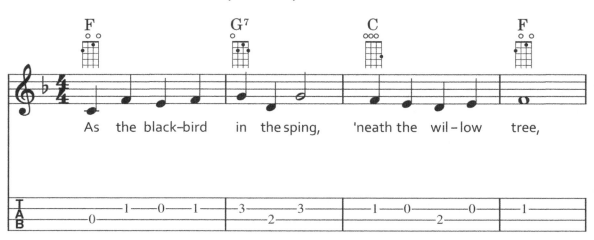

As the black-bird in the sping, 'neath the wil-low tree,

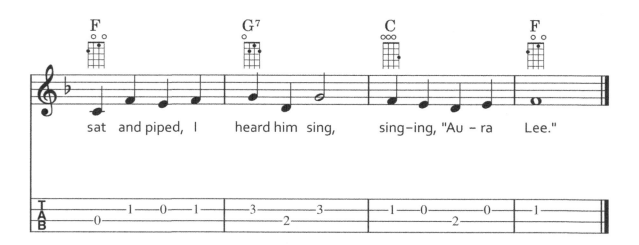

sat and piped, I heard him sing, sing-ing, "Au - ra Lee."

iTS RAINING, iTS POURING

Its rain – ing, its pour – ring. The old man is snor – ing. He bumped his head and went to bed, and could not get up til morn – ing!

HAPPY BIRTHDAY

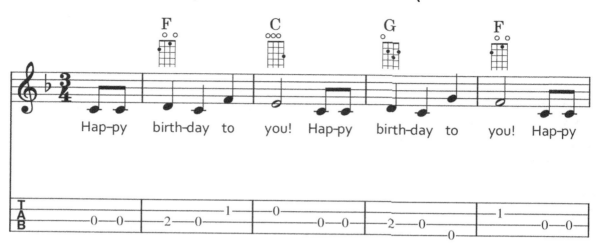

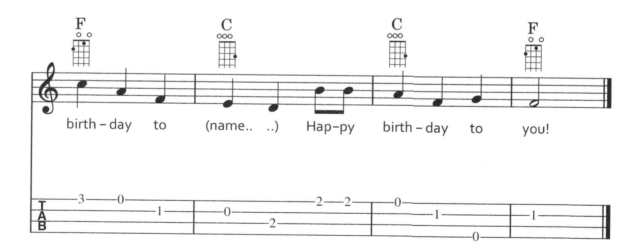

RING AROUND THE ROSIE

Ring a ring a ros – ies, a pock – et

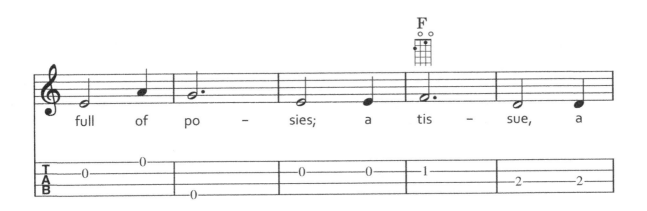

full of po – sies; a tis – sue, a

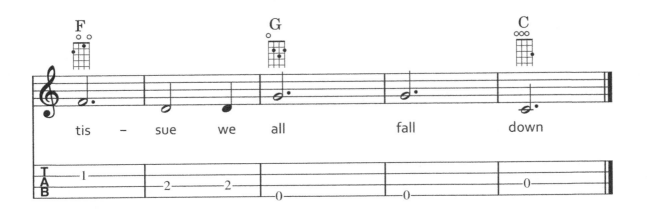

tis – sue we all fall down

TWINKLE, TWINKL,E LITTLE STAR

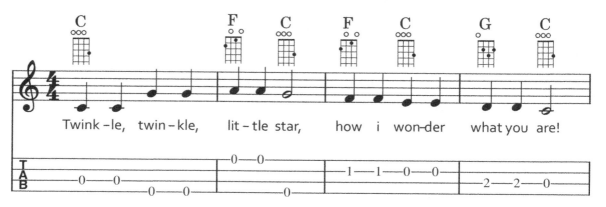

Twink –le,   twin –kle,   lit –tle star,   how   i   won–der   what you   are!

Up   a –bove the   world so   high,   like   a   dia–mond   in   the sky.

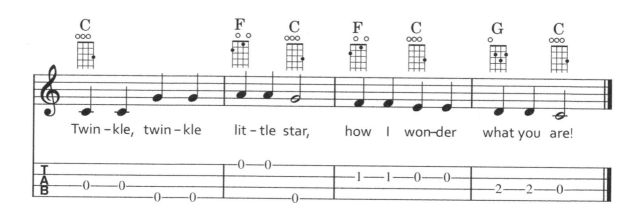

Twin –kle,   twin –kle   lit –tle star,   how   I   won–der   what you   are!

BAA BAA BLACK SHEEP

Baa, baa, black sheep, have you a – ny wool? Yes sir, yes sir,

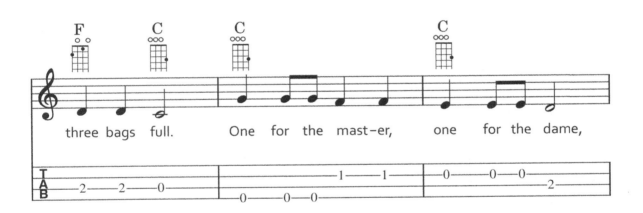

three bags full. One for the mast–er, one for the dame,

one for the lit – tle boy who lives down the lane.

10

MARY HAD A LITTLE LAMB

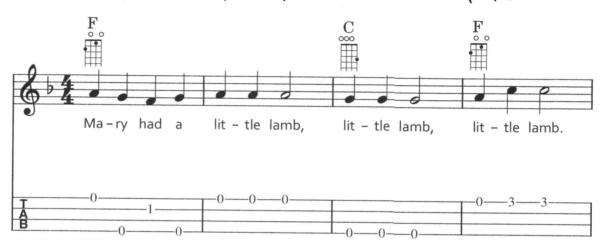

Ma-ry had a   lit-tle lamb,   lit-tle lamb,   lit-tle lamb.

Ma-ry had a   lit-tle lamb its   fleece as white as   snow.

ODE TO JOY

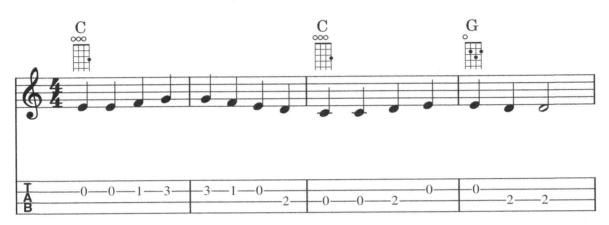

HOT CROSS BUNS

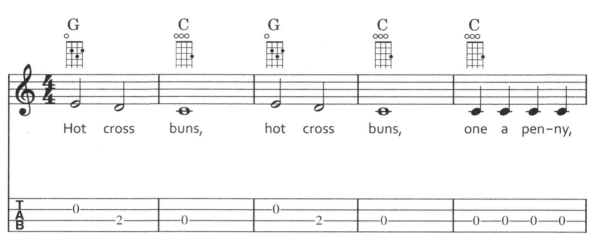

Hot cross buns, hot cross buns, one a pen-ny,

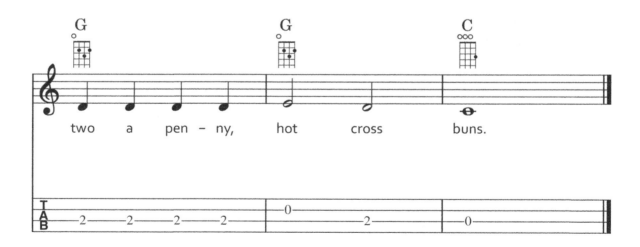

two a pen - ny, hot cross buns.

13

LONDON BRIDGE

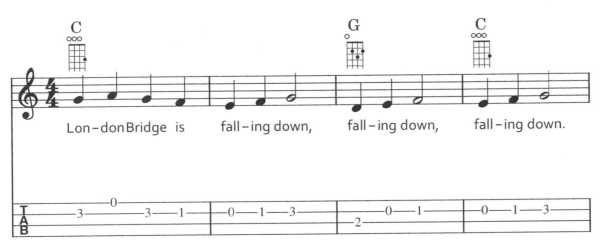

Lon-don Bridge is   fall-ing down,   fall-ing down,   fall-ing down.

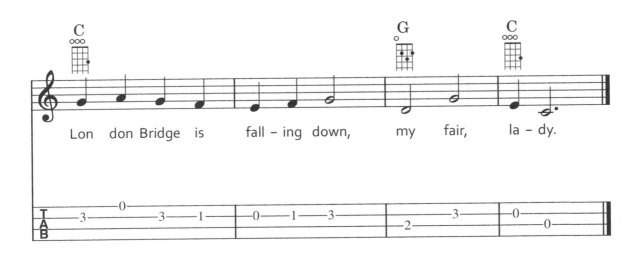

Lon don Bridge is   fall - ing down,   my   fair,   la - dy.

OLD MACDONALD

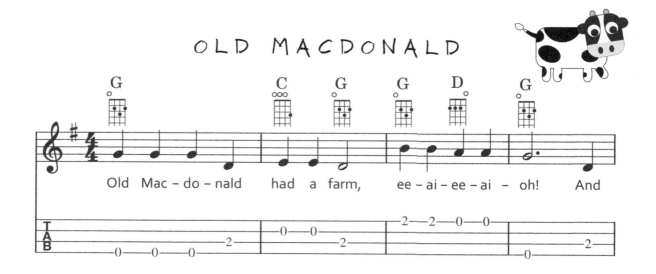

Old Mac - do - nald had a farm, ee - ai - ee - ai - oh! And

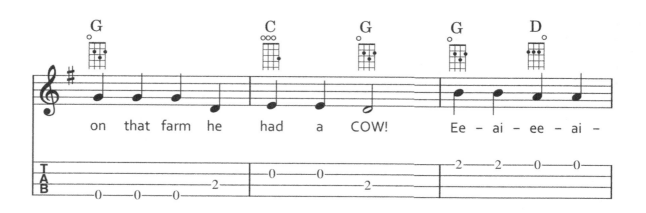

on that farm he had a COW! Ee - ai - ee - ai -

oh! With a moo moo here, moo moo there,

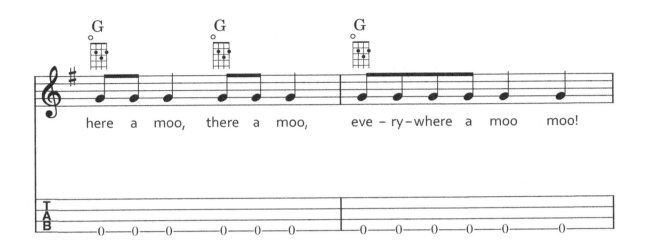

here a moo, there a moo, eve – ry–where a moo   moo!

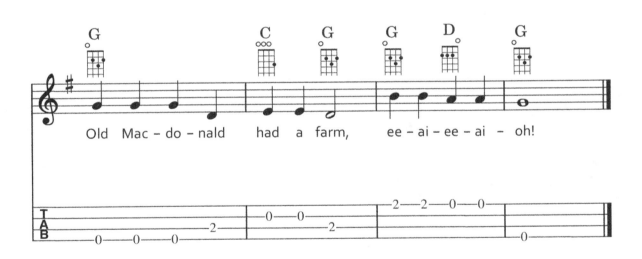

Old Mac – do – nald   had a farm,   ee – ai – ee – ai – oh!

YANKEE DOODLE

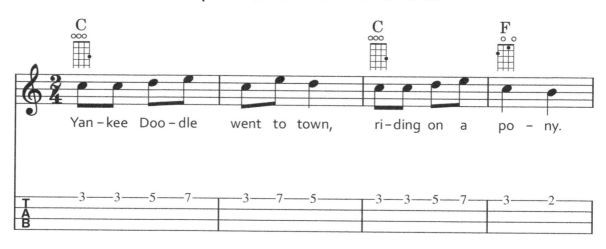

Yan-kee Doo-dle went to town, ri-ding on a po - ny.

Stuck a fea-ther in his hat and called it ma-ca - ro ni.

SKIP TO MY LOU

ARE YOU SLEEPING

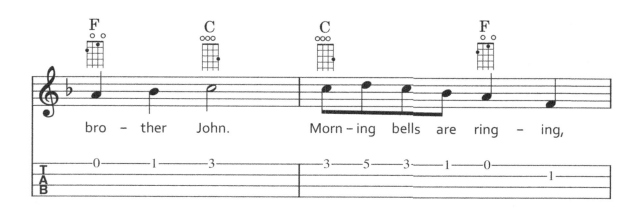

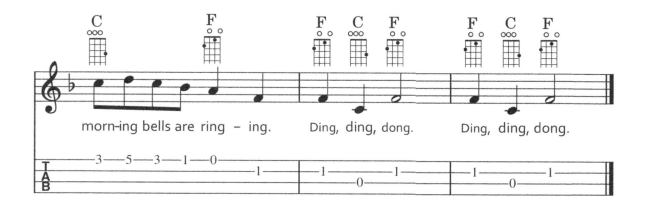

WHEELS ON THE BUS

The wheels on the bus go 'round and 'round,

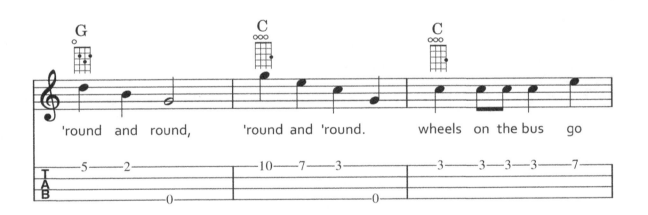

'round and round, 'round and 'round. wheels on the bus go

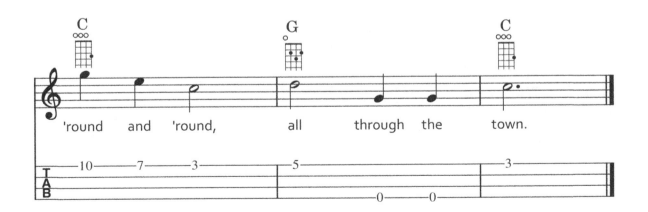

'round and 'round, all through the town.

20

MUFFIN MAN

Do you know the muf – fin man, the muf- fin man the

muf – fin man? Do you know the muf – fin man who

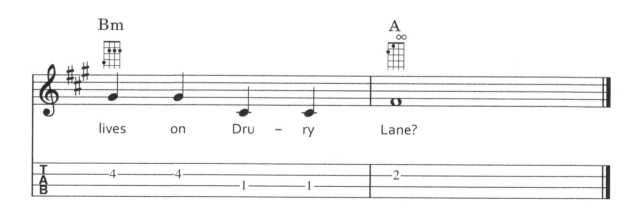

lives on Dru – ry Lane?

21

BINGO

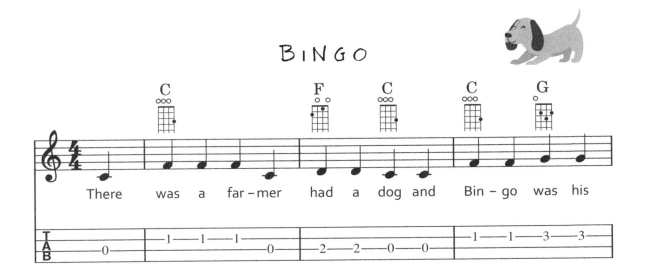

There was a far-mer had a dog and Bin-go was his

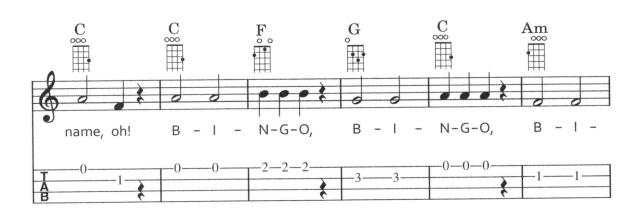

name, oh! B - I - N-G-O, B - I - N-G-O, B - I -

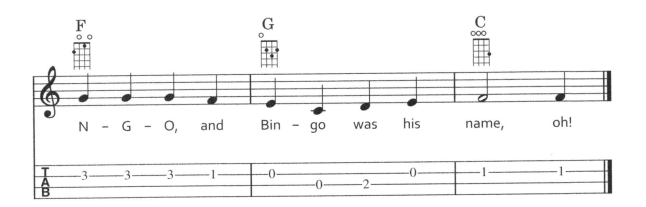

N - G - O, and Bin-go was his name, oh!

ROCK A BYE BABY

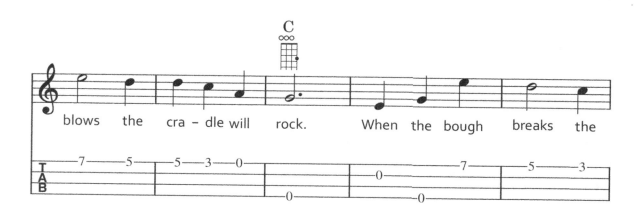

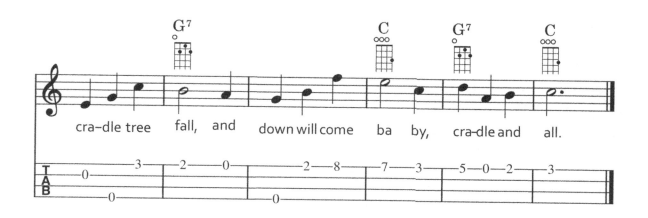

MULBERRY BUSH

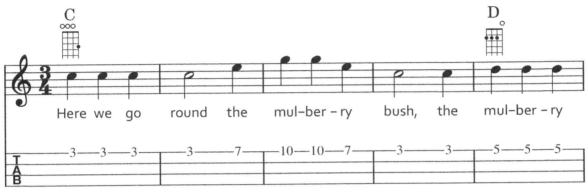

Here we go round the mul-ber-ry bush, the mul-ber-ry

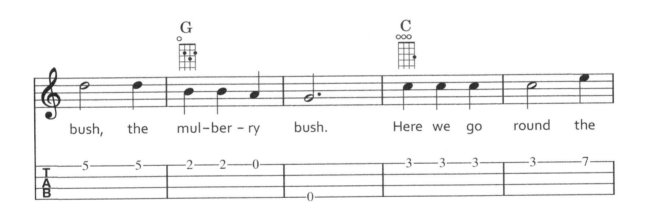

bush, the mul-ber-ry bush. Here we go round the

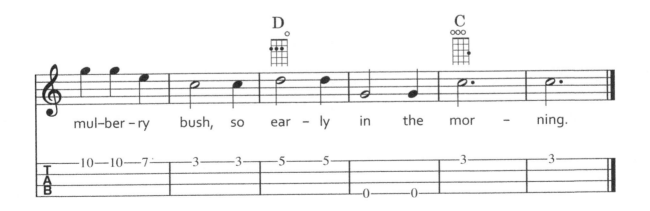

mul-ber-ry bush, so ear-ly in the mor — ning.

 # POP GOES THE WEASEL

All a - round the mul-ber-ry bush, the mon-key chased the

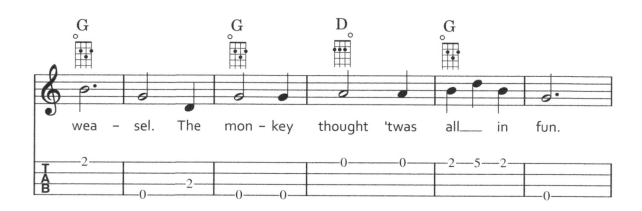

wea - sel. The mon - key thought 'twas all___ in fun.

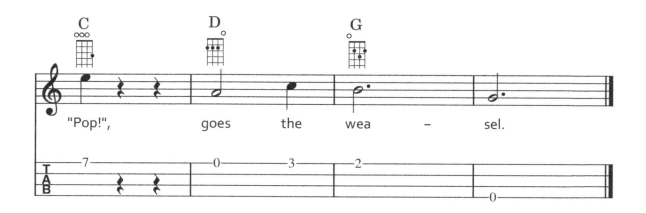

"Pop!", goes the wea - sel.

25

ROW YOUR BOAT

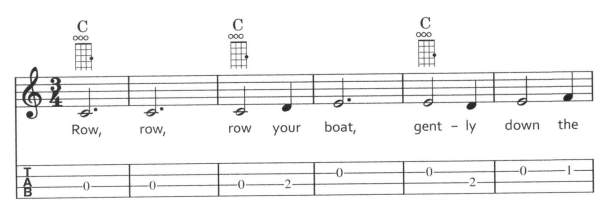

Row, row, row your boat, gent – ly down the

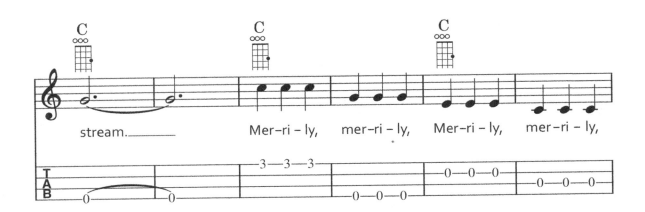

stream._____ Mer–ri – ly, mer–ri – ly, Mer–ri – ly, mer–ri – ly,

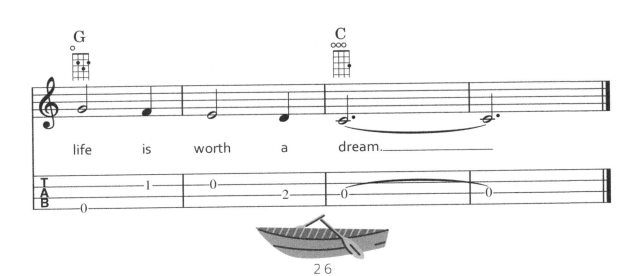

life is worth a dream._____

26

ITSY BITSY SPIDER

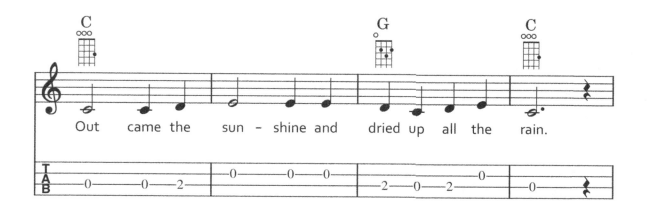

It – sy bit – sy   spi – der climbed   up   the spout   a –   gain.

HEY DIDDLE DIDDLE

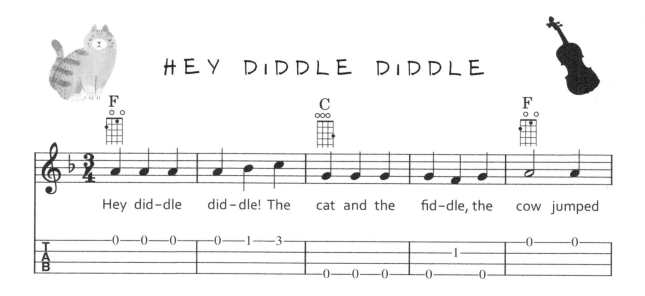

Hey did-dle did-dle! The cat and the fid-dle, the cow jumped

o-ver the moon._____ The lit-tle dog laughed to see such

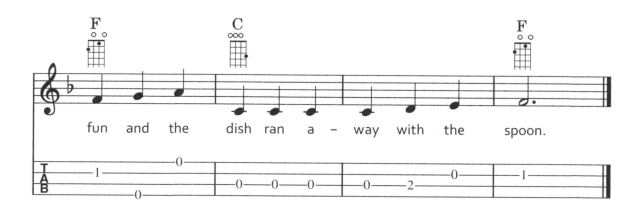

fun and the dish ran a – way with the spoon.

LAVENDER'S BLUE

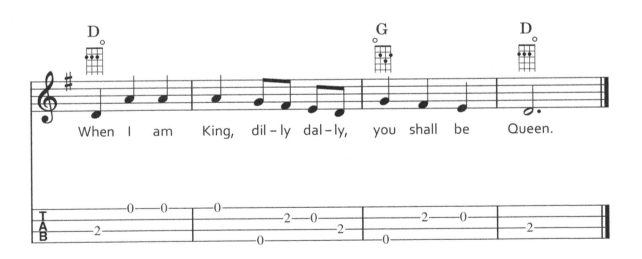

HEADS SHOULDERS KNEES AND TOES

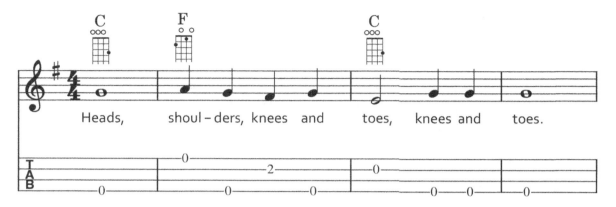

Heads, shoul–ders, knees and toes, knees and toes.

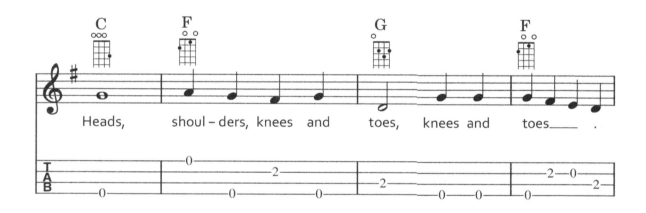

Heads, shoul–ders, knees and toes, knees and toes___ .

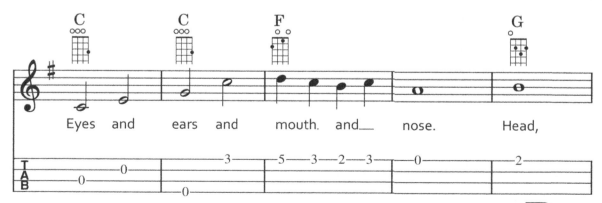

Eyes and ears and mouth. and__ nose. Head,

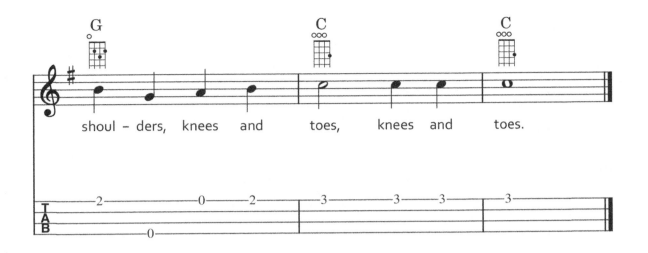

shoul – ders, knees and toes, knees and toes.

JINGLE BELLS

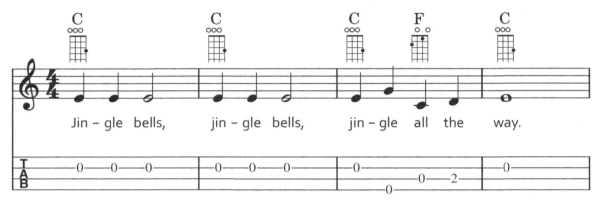

Jin – gle bells, jin – gle bells, jin – gle all the way.

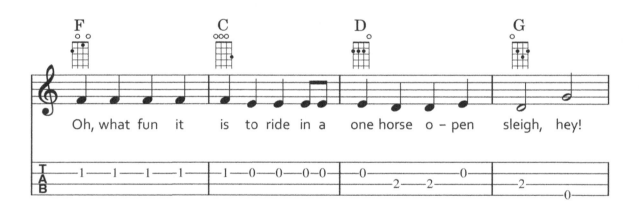

Oh, what fun it is to ride in a one horse o – pen sleigh, hey!

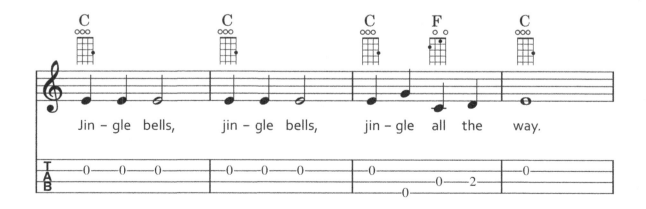

Jin – gle bells, jin – gle bells, jin – gle all the way.

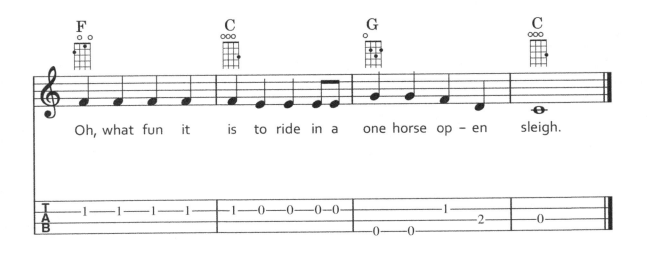

Oh, what fun it is to ride in a one horse op – en sleigh.

LiTTLE BO PEEP

Lit – tle Bo Peep has lost her sheep and does – n't know

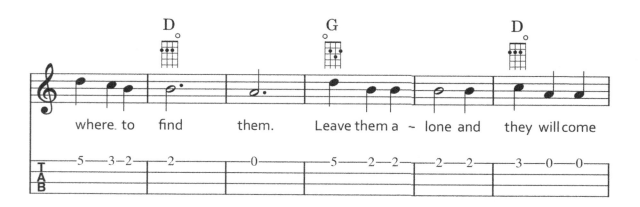

where. to find them. Leave them a – lone and they will come

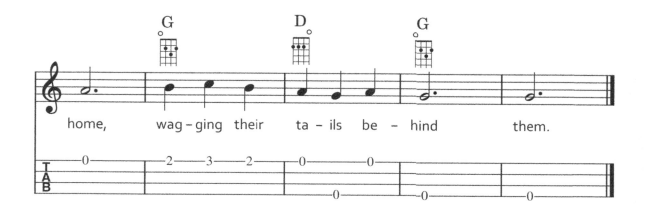

home, wag – ging their ta – ils be – hind them.

POLLY PUT THE KETTLE ON

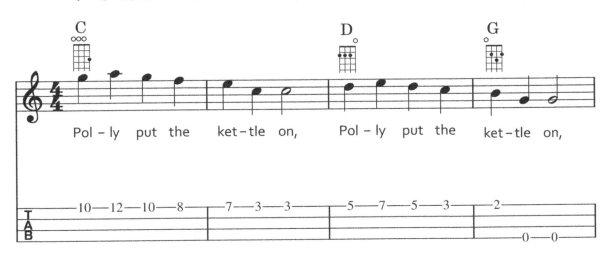

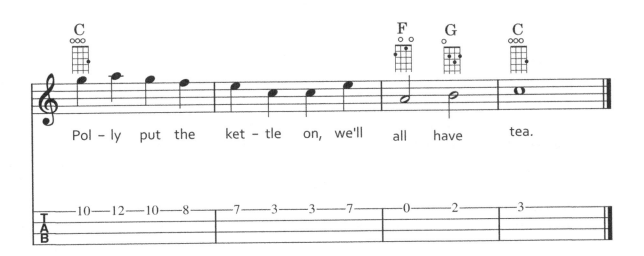

36

FiVE LiTTLE DUCKS

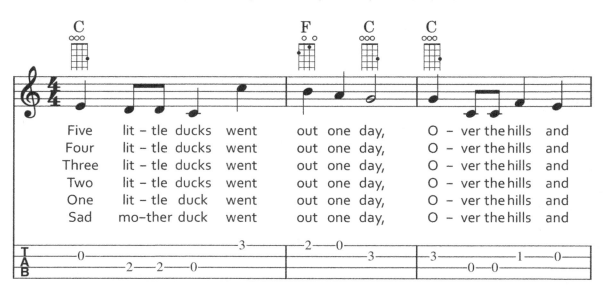

Five lit – tle ducks went out one day, O – ver the hills and
Four lit – tle ducks went out one day, O – ver the hills and
Three lit – tle ducks went out one day, O – ver the hills and
Two lit – tle ducks went out one day, O – ver the hills and
One lit – tle duck went out one day, O – ver the hills and
Sad mo-ther duck went out one day, O – ver the hills and

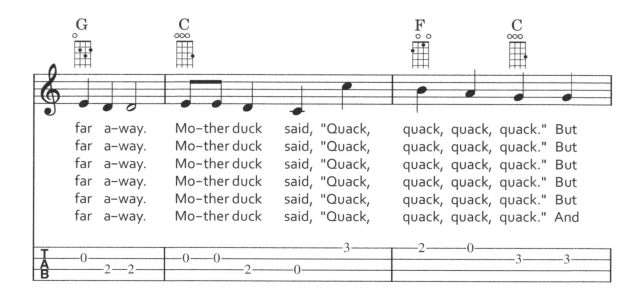

far a–way. Mo-ther duck said, "Quack, quack, quack, quack." But
far a–way. Mo-ther duck said, "Quack, quack, quack, quack." But
far a–way. Mo-ther duck said, "Quack, quack, quack, quack." But
far a–way. Mo-ther duck said, "Quack, quack, quack, quack." But
far a–way. Mo-ther duck said, "Quack, quack, quack, quack." But
far a–way. Mo-ther duck said, "Quack, quack, quack, quack." And

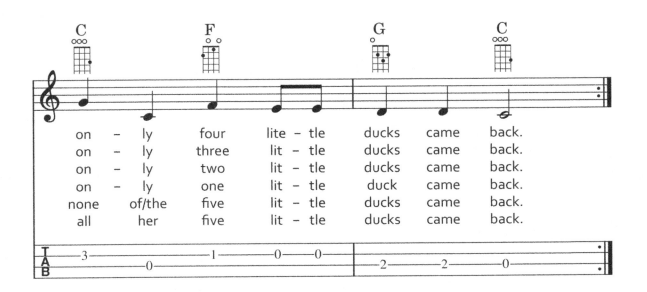

on – ly	four	lite – tle	ducks	came	back.
on – ly	three	lit – tle	ducks	came	back.
on – ly	two	lit – tle	ducks	came	back.
on – ly	one	lit – tle	duck	came	back.
none of/the	five	lit – tle	ducks	came	back.
all her	five	lit – tle	ducks	came	back.

AU CLAIRE DE LA LUNE

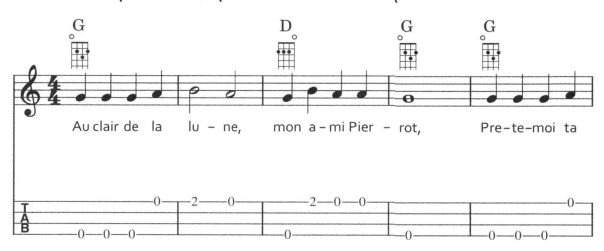

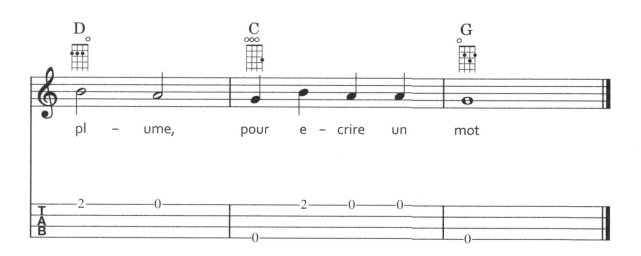

Au Claire De La Lune lyric translation:

In the light of the moon, Pierrot, my friend
Loan me your pen to write something down
My candle's dead, I've got no flame to light it
Open your door, for the love of God!

LiTTLE JACK HORNER

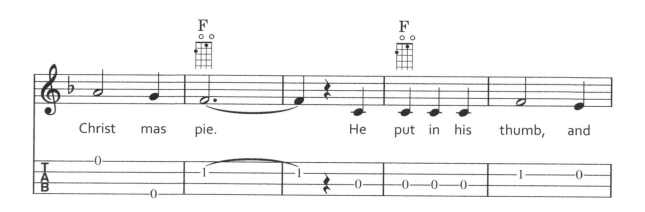

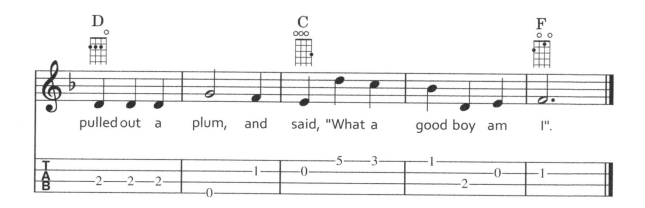

AMAZING GRACE

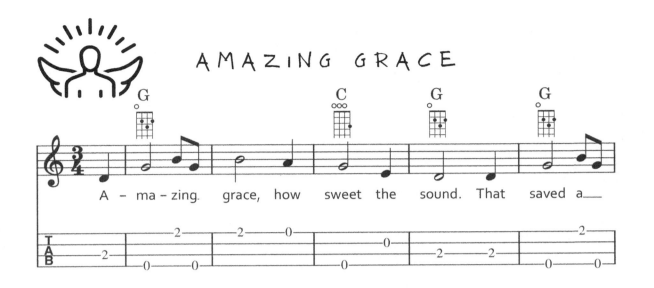

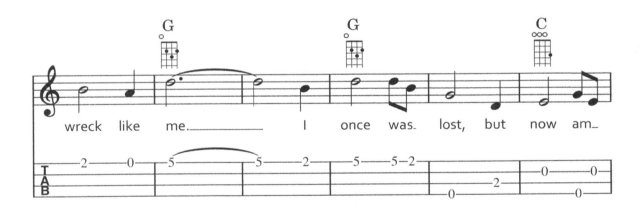

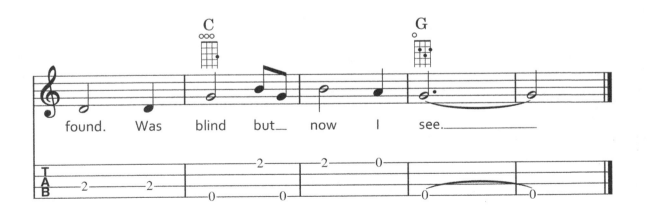

A SAILOR WENT TO SEA

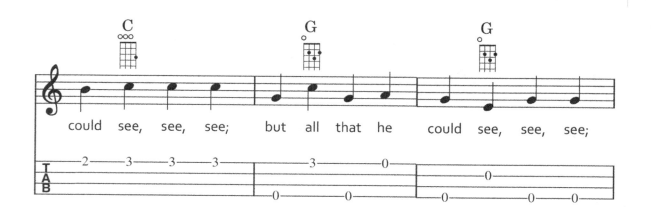

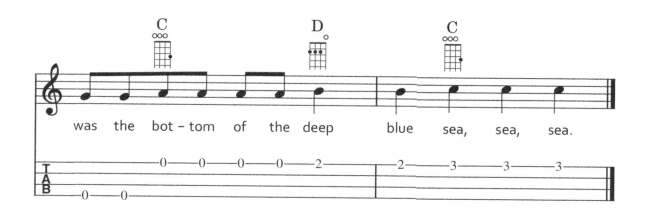

CAN CAN

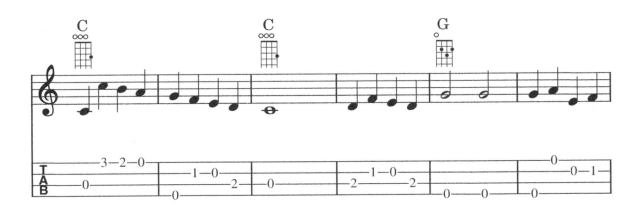

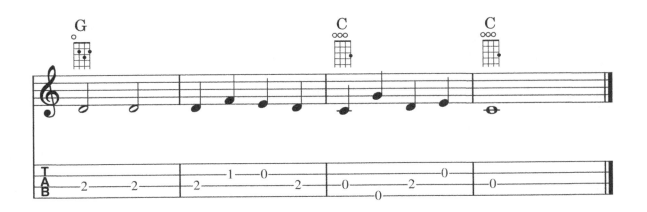

I'M A LITTLE TEAPOT

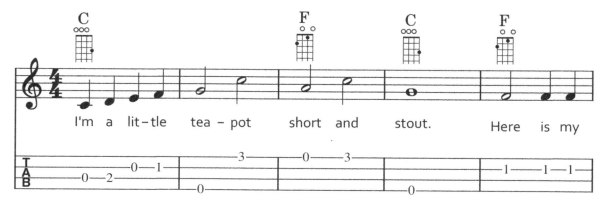

I'm a lit-tle tea-pot short and stout. Here is my

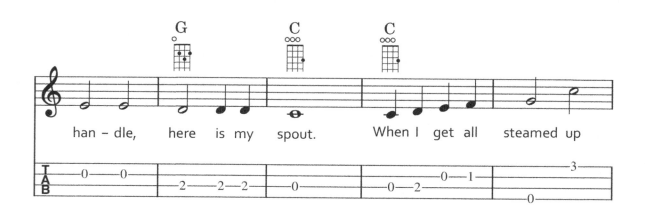

han - dle, here is my spout. When I get all steamed up

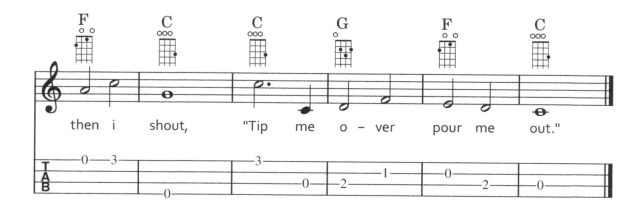

then i shout, "Tip me o - ver pour me out."

ROCK A BYE BABY

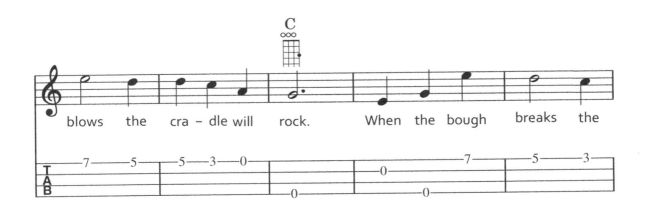

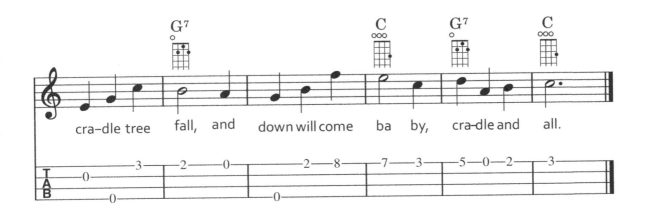

IF YOU'RE HAPPY AND YOU KNOW IT

If you're hap – py and you know it   clap your hands!

Made in the USA
Monee, IL
02 December 2022

19280886R00031